SHATTERED DEGREES

Michael Massanelli

MASSANELLI

Table of contents

1	MY KINGDOM	1
2	RAINBOWS AND BUTTERFLIES	3
3	TAKE MY FEAR	4
4	HOW CAN IT BE	6
5	RAPTURE	8
6	GROWING UP	10
7	PERFECT	12
8	EVERYDAY LIFE	14
9	LIGHT THE CANDLES	16
10	KEEP ME FOCUSED	18
11	READ THE BOOK	21
12	TEARS OF MY PAST	25
13	WHAT DID YOU EXPECCT	29
14	STONE ROLLED BACK	33
15	NOS	37
16	GOD MOM	41
17	AM I DREAMING	44
18	PAST	46
19	JACKSON MISSISSIPPI	49
20	RESPECT MYSELF	52
21	TAPS	54
22	NOT OF THIS WORLD	55
23	YOUR WILL	57
24	ANGEL VS DEMON	59
25	DOVE TO THE DEVIL	61

Table of contents

26 WORTH THE CLIMB.......................... 63
27 LET GO.. 64
28 DARKNESS.................................... 68
29 PLEDGE ALLEGIANCE...................... 69
30 FROM THE INSIDE......................... 70
31 WHILE IT LASTS............................. 72
32 WANT TO GO................................. 74
33 SATAN VS JESUS............................ 77
34 HOLDING ON................................. 81
35 TEMPORARY.................................. 84
36 THE BIBLE IS A LIE......................... 87
37 LET'EM RIDE................................. 92
38 LET IT BE YOURS............................ 94
39 WHAT'S WRONG............................. 97
40 WAR... 100
41 MAN ON A MISSION....................... 102
42 WAITING..................................... 104
43 CAN'T HELP BUT WONDER.............. 107
44 BRING IT ALL DOWN....................... 110
45 SWEET LOVE................................. 112
46 FRACTIONED TIME......................... 114
47 PERCEPTION................................. 116
48 LAY IT ALL OUT............................. 117
49 THE VIOLATED............................... 119
50 I CAN'T....................................... 120

Table of contents

51 ROLLERCOASTER.................................. 121

52 LET ME OUT.. 123

53 MY TIME... 124

54 LET ME SLEEP..................................... 125

55 NOTHING.. 127

56 WHEN THE RAIN COMES..................... 129

57 THINGS IN LIFE................................... 131

58 OLD AND GREY................................... 132

59 NOT MY INTENTION............................ 133

60 MILESTONES....................................... 135

SHATTERED

Shattered does not mean helpless, and broken does not mean useless. They may change how something is viewed or used at any moment, but there is always hope...putting the pieces back together, finding the right part, or just changing perspective all take time and a little **TLC**. **T**ender touch to a physical or emotional need, **L**oving understanding that it may be harder for someone else to get something than it is for you, and **C**are to see something through even though it may be challenging. When something you love is broken it can easily be replaced or repaired but when someone you love is broken it can be way more challenging...but love them the way you want to be loved and forgive them the way you would want to be forgiven.

MY KINGDOM

Be not afraid
They'll come by night
to carry me away
One will deny,
another betray
and cast Me away

Be not afraid
The wages of sin
I must now go pay
Angels will come
and roll the stone away
it's the beginning,
beginning of the end

My kingdom is not from here
My kingdom

The cross can't diminish
Don't let your heart concern
My job now here is finished
But soon I shall return

Be not afraid
The wages of sin
I must now go pay
Angels will come
and roll the stone away
it's the beginning,
beginning of the end

My kingdom is not from here
My kingdom

The cross can't diminish
Don't let your heart concern
My job now here is finished
But soon I shall return

Will you follow
Will you let go
Born again for salvation
There's only one way
to the Father
There'll never be another
Many will come though
To deceive you
So I ask you
Will you follow

The cross can't diminish
Don't let your heart concern
My job now here is finished
But soon I shall return

Soon I shall return
Like a thief
I will rerun

RAINBOWS & BUTTERFLIES

Rainbows and butterflies
Are how we would like life to be,
If life were always bright & colorful though
Nothing would ever test our integrity.
But if we think about it a little more
Our life really is rainbows & butterflies,
We may have a storm that beats us down but
Something pulls us through to be the more wise.
A Rainbow is a promise God gave
Never to flood the world again with water,
Divinely engineered with a greater cause and purpose
Bringing it all together like he did with us at the altar.
Unfortunately, it does take some darkness
To allow the light to brighter shine,
Though for the butterfly to fly it must
Endure a greater darkness within its woven twine.
Realizing, as a caterpillar, it has a greater role
Freely giving up what it knows committing to a greater goal.
Letting its guard down and asking God to do the rest,
Inwardly maturing and growing to better fly a quest.
Everyday we have a choice to overcome trials we may face,
So lets spread our wings and make this world a better place.

TAKE MY FEAR

There's a burden on my mind that brings me down
Heavy on my mind and pulls me down
It's been so long, not sure what to do
Make it go away, please far away

I long for the day there's no more pain
When I feel I can wash it all away
I'm going to need your help
To make it go away, so far away
Will you take my hand
Help me to my feet

I need you to be here with me
I need your strength here with me
Will you ease my fear, please
Take my fear, be near, be here

Freedom in forgiveness I heard someone say
They say you can take it all the way
I'm going to put my trust in you
To take it all the way, all away
All this pain
All this fear

I need you to be here with me
I need your strength here with me
Will you ease my fear, please
I can't do this on my own
don't want to be alone
Can't do this on my own
Take my fear, be near, be here
I can't do this on my own

Thank you Lord for delivering me
It took some work but I'm finally free
I can't thank you enough
For taking it all away, all way

You gave me the strength to be free
No more pain in me
And forgive me Lord
For trying on my own

Thank you for delivering me
Hallelujah, I'm finally free
Can't thank you enough
For taking it all away, all way

HOW CAN IT BE

From what there was
to what's to come
You have it all
Under control
You came to die
Then three days later
Beyond the grave
You saved my soul

You have
no beginning
and no end
Never ending
Eternity
So many question
I have to ponder
and I wonder
How can it be

How can it be
You even love me
How can it be
You know my name
How can it be
You can even change me
How can it be
I'll never be the same

You have the power to create
You have the power to take away
We've let you down so many times
You could turn your back but yet you stay

How can it be
Oh I wonder
How can it be

How can it be
I'm here to ponder
And I wonder
How can it be

How can it be
You even love me
How can it be
You know my name
How can it be
You can even change me
How can it be
I'll never be the same

RAPTURE

For those who are ready
may they be ready to go
For those who are not
may you forever know

You all had your chance
You all had a voice
You all were warned
You all made your choice

Some will get a second
chance to be redeemed
A lot will suffer worse
than they've ever dreamed

The World will not have ended
but it will not be the same
You'll dread the day
you realize it's not just a game

Believe or don't but whether
you want it to or not
The world is going to bite you
and hurt quite a lot

The world is servant
to The Word that's true
Time is running out
and stopping it you cannot do

Your soul is more important
than all the things you've owned
You can't keep them anyways
so why not have your sins atoned

Yeshua HaMashiach
better known as Jesus H Christ
Will save you from your sin
and defeat the Devil on his pillaging heist

Your soul is being fought for
in a realm you cannot see
The winner takes all
and keeps it for all eternity

Stop playing around
and taking your life for granted
Wake up to reality
and stop pretending it's enchanted

Fantasy land can be fun to visit
every now and then
But this stuff is real
and when it ends ya don't know when

It only takes a moment
to take the time to confess
God came here as a man
and died to save us from this mess

Take His hand since
He reached His out for you
Take the leap of faith
because there's no work you can do

Heaven can't be earned
and you won't get out of life alive
There's a Judgment Day coming so
make sure Heaven is ready for you to arrive

GROWING UP

Looking up to
the hands that feed
Hoping they give
all I need
I'm not long in the world
but a miracle to be
A long road ahead
and so much to see

Slow down child
you're growing to fast
Enjoy your youth
it won't last
Your time will come
you'll get to do your part
and pains will find you
and break your heart

I wish I could say
I'm perfect and know what to do
but I know I'm not
and not fair how it harms you

If only growing up and getting older
meant wising up and getting smarter
Mistakes wouldn't keep
showing up
You'll see when you're older
So now just enjoy
Growing up

One can't Keep the peace
without being a little snappy
Impossible to keep
everyone always happy
You can only do what seems best
pray for the good and hope to forget the rest

Sometimes it takes
giving up
the past you're holding
Breaking up
The fearful molding
Looking forward and
Stepping up
With all the stuff unfolding
Gotta reach down deep
and turn it up

The mistakes that we make
The bruises we take
Learning the difference
between the real and the fake
it's all part of growing up
Just a part of growing up

We can be gripped with fear
and hurt those dear
and wonder why
things can't be clear
it's all part of growing up
Just a part of growing up

PERFECT

In an imperfect world
how can a perfect
person even exist?
A person without a flaw, a flag,
or even a twist.

Even if this person existed
and you were able to find
Wondering what they are hiding
would always rattle the mind.

However, the perfect person does exist
and not too hard to find
once you start using the
right definition in your mind.

Knowing perfect
does not mean perfection
is your biggest step
in the right direction.

Perfection is without a flaw
in any kind of way
Perfect is the rain
on a hot drought filled day.

You may have a weakness
where someone else is strong
or you have strength
to help the weak along.

They may know something
that you don't
or you may be willing to take a stand
on something they won't.

You may both have the same hurts
but like the same things
or have a similar messed up past
but willing to see what the future brings.

Stop looking for perfection since
you're not even close to it
and look for someone to give you balance
to a perfect fit.

EVERYDAY LIFE

Everyday life
has enough trouble of its own;
Everyday life
throws another sin to atone.
If everyday strife
could be clearly shown
then everyday strife
would be left alone.

You know what you know
and that's the best ya got;
Your opinion of me
doesn't meant squat.
So take your advice
and your opinions too;
no need for me to say it
you know what you can do.

Who are you to judge?
Don't judge me!
Who are you to think
you know me?
Who are you to cast
your curse on me?
Who are you...
but a fool too blind to see!

I feel sorry for you pundits
who can't comprehend;
To Hell you hypocrites
with your immoral bend.
Your boasting ego trips
in your ignorant feeble mind,
Your delusional warped reality
boozed up is the best you can find.

So sick of your crap;
so wish I could be
The one to set you straight
this side of eternity.
But I'll let go
of how you strike a nerve,
Either here or there
you'll get what you deserve.

Who are you to judge?
Don't judge me!
Who are you to think
you know me?
Who are you to cast
your curse on me?
Who are you...
but a fool too blind to see!

LIGHT THE CANDLES

Just when we thought
we might have it figured out
Just as we thought
we knew what life's about
Just when we thought
we knew it all for sure
Tragedy strikes and
it becomes obscure

Life has a way
just when we think all is well
To turn it all around
and put us through hell
Some deaths seem senseless
and some seem deserved
some life needs ending
and some needs preserved
As we gather together
to mourn this loss
Let's remember the meaning
behind the Cross

Light the candles
Bow your head in prayer
Light the candles
For the loss we share
Light the candles
It's hard to bare
but light the candles

In birth we learn to love
In loss we learn to live
In sorrow we learn to hurt
In need we learn to give

Light the candles

In giving we learn empathy
In peace we learn to heal
In war we learn to survive
In pain we learn to feel

Light the candles

Life is funny
and often unfair
Meaning is based
on how much we care
When all is well
life is great
When it falls a part
it's a burdened weight
If we could really connect
with love and ambitions
Unconditional love wouldn't
come with certain conditions

Light the candles
Bow your head in prayer
Light the candles
For the loss we share
Light the candles
It's hard to bear
but light the candles

KEEP ME FOCUSED

I am so not a part
of this world we know
I do my part
but what's to show
The Word is clear
can only be one love
The world before us
or the God above

From time to time
I lose my way
And it's hard to make it
to the end of the day
I really do
want to do what's right
Give me strength
restore my sight

Keep me focused
focused
Keep me focused on you
In your promise
Your purpose
Be faithful and true
Keep me focused
Focused
Keep me focused on You
I'm going to need your help
to pull me through

There are days when I feel
I could rule the world
but days I need
to be uncurled
I wish I could say
My future is bright
Right now I need you
Give me strength to fight

Keep me focused
focused
Keep me focused on you
In your promise
Your purpose
Be faithful and true
Keep me focused
Focused
Keep me focused on You
I'm going to need your help
to pull me through

Keep me focused while I'm here
Cuz I'm ready to be with you
Keep me focused while I'm here
The gates I wanna walk through
Keep me focused

Keep me focused while I'm here
And the purpose I should be giving
Keep me focused while I'm here
On the life I should be living
Keep me focused

TODAY

READ THE BOOK

When you find yourself asking
what's wrong with the world
how can it be so bad
What's up with all the hatred
why in the world
does it have to be so sad

Know there's a plan that's been laid out
Through the centuries has been Played out
Not one thing left undone
So many people have sold out
So many more wanting to hold out
The end told before it began

We've read the book
We know it ends
Take a good look
Tell all your friends
The end is among us
but be not afraid
A judgment awaits us
Though the debt has been paid
For those who believe
the path has been paved
for those who believe

The Word has been around
since the Creator of time
It spells it all out
all of history
A redeemer being punished
without a crime
and a deceiver on the lose with a cunning conspiracy

Go read the book
and tell all your friends
Take a good look
to see how it ends
The end is among us
but be not afraid
A judgment awaits us
Though the debt has been paid
For those who believe
the path has been paved
for those who believe

Every thought
ever deed
Every gift
every greed
A coming judgement awaits

Every word
every prayer
Every curse
every swear
Then off through the gates

Heaven or hell
no in between
It's all loving and fair
even if you think it's mean
Most wont agree and will think it's unjust
but the creator makes the rules
and to be fair He must
Lay it all out and let you choose
It's your soul to gain
it's your soul to lose
Accept or reject it
the debt has still been paid
will you be forever happy
with the choice you made

It's all been paid
for those who believe
it's up to you
you can receive
Give it a chance
set yourself free
Doesn't take much
you can be
With those who believe
debt has been paid
for those who believe

PICTURE PARABLE
TREE OF KNOWLEDGE
of GOOD & EVIL

TEARS OF MY PAST

Every now and then
I'm reminded of who
The Who I used to be
Reminded of things
I used to do
and it brings me to my knees

I wish I could go back
and undo some things
but how would it change me now
Better or worse
there's no way to know
but gotta get past it some how
-Lord will you show me how

When the tears of my past
creep up on me
I get down on my knees and pray
And the fears of my past
flee from me
as the Lord washes them away
-The Lord washes them away

I need to learn
the lessons from them
and try not to do them again
But I know I'm not perfect
again, I will fail
it's just a matter of when

I'll try my best
to hold my head high
knowing the truth sets me free
Doing what's right
and staying on track
to fulfill my destiny
-when the past comes looking for me

When the tears of my past
creep up on me
I get down on my knees and pray
And the fears of my past
flee from me
as the Lord washes them away
-The Lord washes them away

Being a child of God
doesn't mean I won't hurt
or that I won't bring pain
Just saved by grace
a sinner by birth
awaiting the eternal reign

It's a temporary past
it won't forever last
here and gone it's all temporary
The times is coming
I too will be like my past
just another old faded memory
-An old faded memory

When the tears of my past
creep up on me
I get down on my knees and pray
And the fears of my past
flee from me
as the Lord washes them away
-The Lord washes them away
Please Lord wash them all away

I TRY

I BECAUSE

I CARE

WHAT DID YOU EXPECT

Take away God
take away prayer
society withering away
babies slaughtered without a care
what do you expect

Genders changing
a moral decay
evil abounds
when you take the Bible away
What do you expect

What do you expect
when you turn your back
on the one who died
but then came back
The rules He gave
were to protect us all
we let Him go
and down we fall
What do you expect
What do you expect

The Bible told of rulers to come
yet we toss it aside and grow numb
a time of a great knowledge explosion
along with a great society implosion
What do you expect

It tells us a cashless society will emerge
and people will kill to scratch an erg
A mark would come for all to take
just look around for goodness sake

Cards and chips replacing cash
headlines worsening people acting rash
Rejecting where you come from
careless where you're going
Christians already being beheaded
Revelation blood already flowing
What do you expect

What do you expect
when you turn your back
on the one who died
but then came back
The rules He gave
were to protect us all
we let Him go
and down we fall
What do you expect
What do you expect

When the leader of the free world
addresses a new world order is upon us
What do you expect
Then his son comes in as a leader too
knowing the towers were hit without a fuss
What do you expect

A beast will come to cause an image to speak
Two witness will come and their death all will seek
Holographic artist being brought back to life
and the world thinks the Christians are causing the strife

A war is coming
where the great nation will fall
The drums beating loud
while gathering troops await the call
It's all been planned
It's all been told
But you ignore it all
as your heart grows cold
What do you expect

When you turn your back
What do you expect
When the truth you reject
What do you expect

Deny your creator
What do you expect
When of the Word you are a hater
What do you expect

PICTURE PARABLE
COMPASSIONATE HEART

STONE ROLLED BACK

A child is born
under the bright lit star,
To a journey hard
but outreach far.
He would teach them well
but they would receive Him not,
By Heaven and Hell
was the crucifixion plot.

The crowd roared (Drum the seat)...
Give Barabbas back (Clap 1x)
As the crowd roared (drum)...
The whips slashed His back (C 1x)
Across is back (Clap 2x)

They nailed Him up
though He did no wrong,
Living as a man
but God all along.
It is finished, the last He spoke,
then the world, suddenly awoke.

And the ground rolled (Drum)...
And the veil cracked (C 1x)
As the ground rolled (Drum)...
They knew there's no turning back (C 1x)
No turning back (C 2x)

They had pierced the Lord
deep in His side;
but his job was done,
had already died.
All part of the plan,
right on track;
He gave His Word,
He would be back.

And the thunder rolled (Drum)...
At the lightening crack (C 1x)
When the thunder roared (drum)..
The stone rolled back (C 1x)
The stone rolled back (C 2x)

And in that tomb
He came back to life;
the heavenly groom
the church, His wife.
When his head fell down
the sky turned black
God lit up the sky (Drum)...
when the stone rolled back (C 1x)
The stone rolled away (Drum)...
with a lightening crack (C 2x)

The angels await
to let the trumpets sound,
The King of Kings
He's been crowned.
Few believed He was the Lord;
Doubt no more, He brings the sword.

The horses ride (Drum)...
As the sky rolls back (Cx1)
His voice of thunder rolls (Drum)...
He's now coming back (Cx1)
The Saints coming back (Cx2)

CODED CRITTERS
FROG
Forever Rely On God

PROVERBS 3:5

NOS

You people are sheeple
so easy to deceive
We can lie to your face
yet you still believe
Our society was secret
yet hidden in sight
threw out all the good
and called evil right
Step by step
we gave you false hope
In the epitome of evil
You call him the Pope
Bring us your kids
and your money too
You're pawns in our game
nothing you can do

To stop
novus
ordo
seclorum
The novus ordo seclorum

A new world order
the agenda before us
We can throw it in your face
you still can't stop us
A plan this big
all takes some time
Pretending that we care
is our only crime

We left our land
to conquer more
No stone unturned
we couldn't explore
Pretending we are others
just part of the game
and killing our own people
just to ruin their name
So many tombstones
and unmarked graves
All your land was free
cuz we killed all the Braves

To start the
novus
ordo
seclorum
The novus ordo seclorum

You can't stop the
novus
ordo
seclorum
The novus ordo seclorum

Thank you for your help
couldn't do it on our own
novus ordo seclorum
how you still can't see this
our mind is blown
novus ordo seclorum

Carry on all slave labor
or we'll give you the axe
Continue on thinking you are free
as we inflate your tax
Keep up the good work
fighting amongst yourselves
Our plan all along
while taking Bibles from the shelves

To hide our
Novus Ordo Seclorum

Rock-a-bye all you people
as we lull you to sleep
Only one can stop the wolf
from devouring you sheep
Most reject Him now
while some of you will wait
By the time you wake up
it will be too late

In the age of the
New World Order

Coming soon
Novus Ordo Seclorum

You can't stop
Novus Ordo Seclorum

GOD MOM

Not sure Lord why you've chosen me to be
the vessel to which you come to be with us
It's my honor to do Your Will Lord
no need to question or discuss

I'll be condemned by those around me
because they know I know no man
But I will do whatever I need
gracious to be part of Your plan

I give my life to bring in Yours
may You never have a need
Growing with You will be a gift
what's coming will be great indeed

When I wrap my arms around you
and you feel my love is real
Know I'll be right here for you
no matter how you feel

My love will never change
you can always trust in me my child
Come be what this world needs
and never be defiled

I'll be Lord, who the Prophets say I will be
the vessel needed to reconcile the lost
It's My mission to serve and be The Lord
no need to sorrow at what it will cost

I'll be condemned by those around Me
because they know I'm not just a man
But I will do whatever I need
glorious to be the redeeming plan

I give My life to give you yours
I'll be all you ever need
Dying for you will be My gift
what's coming will be great indeed

When I wrap my arms around you
and you feel My love is real
Know I'm always here for you
no matter how you feel
My love will never change
you can always trust in Me my child
I'll be what this world needs
and never be defiled

(Cont...)

Welcome home child, it's all I said it would be
the vessel pierced upon the cross
Come place your hand in the holes
and see it wasn't a loss

I was crucified by those around Me
resurrection proved I wasn't just a man
My kingdom will have no end
that was all part of the plan

I gave My life to give you yours
never again will you need
Come take part in this eternal gift
your smiles tell Me it's all great indeed

When I wrap my arms around you
and you know My love is real
You see I'm always here for you
no matter how you feel
My love will never change
you can always trust in Me my child
No more pain or worldly needs
and nothing can be defiled

AM I DREAMING

Twinkle of an eye
and everything changes
One body to the next
with the power of God Christ exchanges
Could it really happen to me
now wondering can it really be
Did I just take my first breath in eternity

Pinch me now, am I dreaming
I've believed so many lies
Are you here redeeming
Am I still alive
Pinch me now, am I dreaming
Meeting you in the sky
Because it's seeming
I'm not alive
Am I alive

Everyone around me said it wouldn't happen
Even if it does, give it up cuz nobody knows when
Though here I am not sure what to say,
actually been taken away
We've waited here so long for this day

Pinch me now, am I dreaming
I've believed so many lies
Are you here redeeming
Am I still alive
Pinch me now, am I dreaming

Meeting you in the sky
Because it's seeming
I'm not alive

With you, right here
Is it real or another lie
With you, right here
Wondering if I'm alive

Pinch me now, am I dreaming
I've believed so many lies
Are you here redeeming
Am I still alive
Pinch me now, am I dreaming
Meeting you in the sky
Because it's seeming
I'm not alive

Tell me am I dreaming now
Cuz Lord it's seeming now
I could be dreaming now
Tell me I'm not dreaming now
I'm now alive
Finally alive

PAST

The impossible task
Of forgetting the past
Will continue going on
As long as we last

But the lessons learned
And all the stripes earned
Make it easier
For pages to be turned

Life lessons give and take
If we're real and not fake
They are there to mold us
For our own sake

Do we listen to what they say
Change our minds to a better way
Or throw in the towel
And let them continue to prey

Into this world our folks brought us in
But do not define who we are within
Good and evil always fighting for us
And it's up to us who we let win

Love is much stronger than any hate
Everyone's purpose to each their own fate
Some will get it here now
For others it will be too late

Whatever we're here meant to learn
Which can be different at ever turn
Focus on who you are
Let others be their own concern

Against all enemies I'm here to defend
And proud I get Time to spend
My time with you while we're here
You and I until the end

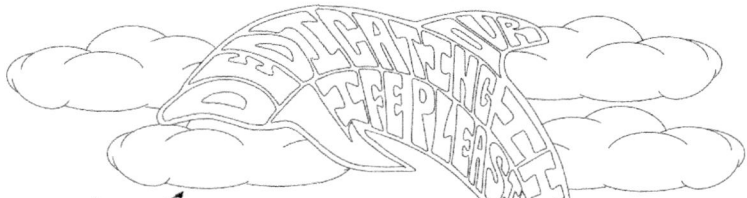

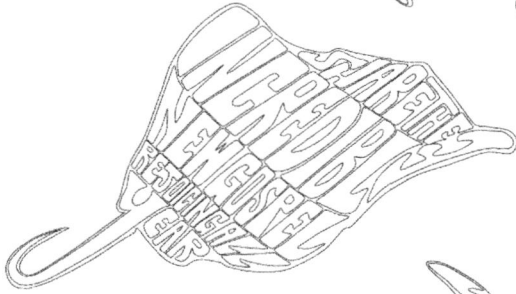

JACKSON MISSISSIPPI

Folks down south live life a little slow
Something those city folks will surely never know
I've seen both sides and I have to say
There's something about a Southern Belle
will take your breath away

Up to the bar I pulled up a chair
A sip of my drink and couldn't help but stare
Her jam came on and the lights dimmed down
Everyone stopped and turned around
She put up her hair and set down her cup
Stepped out on the floor and lit that mother up

She was a smooth moving
eye stunning one of a kind
A heart throbbin jaw droppin
blow your mind

Hips rocking boot stomping
My oh my
Hair teasing quite pleasing
Turn every eye

She had every guy a wooing
she knew what she was doing
Noooo, I never knew what hit me
Down in Jackson Mississippi
so glad that he hit me
down in Jackson Mississippi

Those city girls only wish they knew A thing or two
With their big lips, clip-ons and fingernail glue
Oh This little Belle was a stunning sight
All nat-u-ral such a delight
I'll probably never met another
But why would I Bother
So glad that it hit me
Down in Jackson Mississippi

She was a smooth moving
eye stunning one of a kind
A heart throbbin jaw droppin
blow your mind

Hips rocking boot stomping
My oh my
Hair teasing quite pleasing
Turn every eye

She had every guy a wooing
she knew what she was doing
Noooo, I never knew what hit me
Down in Jackson Mississippi
so glad that he hit me
down in Jackson Mississippi

I never knew what hit me...
Never find this in the city...
So glad that it hit me
Down in Jackson Mississippi

She had every guy a wooing
she knew what she was doing
Smooth moving
eye stunning one of a kind
Hips rocking boot stomping
My oh my
Hair teasing quite pleasing
I'm ready to die
I never knew what hit me
Down in Jackson Mississippi

Oh wow oh wow how could this be
I never knew what hit me
down in Jackson Mississippi

RESPECT MYSELF

Early on we are subject
To the wounds of the past
Left unchecked
Who knows how long they'll last
Our parents recycled what their parents gave
And truths to the matter
all end up in graves

For our own sake we need to learn
how to see through the mess
Being better than they were
Even if they can't confess
How screwed they were
and all the mistakes they made
Whether abusive and controlling
or away and strayed

One thing I need to know
even when there's no one around
I love and respect myself
Even though my past can come
and bring me down
I love and respect myself
Yes, I love and respect myself

They may not have known
how to be better than they were
And if given a chance to ask them
The madness may stir
All the emotions and pain
We all have to share
Being prepared to cry
If I choose to dare

Regardless who they were
even if they are not around
I need to love and respect myself
Even though my past can come
and bring me down
I need love and respect myself
Yes, love and respect myself

Forgiving what they did
So I can get on with my life
I love and respect myself
Letting go of the pain they brought to me
So I can love and respect myself
Yes, so I can love and respect myself

TAPS

Laid to rest
Rest In Peace
May you be
Ever be
With the Lord
God almighty this day
Rest In Peace

NOT OF THIS WORLD

The world in which we live
is full of heartache and pain
Corruption everywhere
enough to drive you insane
Everywhere we turn
it's another attack
Everywhere we go
another monkey on the back

Anyone good
will face this even more
Though if God be with them
they'll learn to soar
We're at war with the world
piercing is the battle drum
And though the world has tried
we have overcome

Be not of this world
with God on the Throne
Not of this world
stand with Christ alone
Not of this world
be not of this world
until the trumpet is blown

The world in which we've made
with the two of us alone
Is a blessing in itself
more than we've ever known
Everywhere we turn
it's another blue line sign
Everywhere we go
proof of masterpiece grand design
.

Our life we have is good
I couldn't ask for anything more
Our God is for us
let Him fight our war
We're at war with the world
piercing is the battle drum
And though the world has tries
we will overcome

Be not of this world
with God on the Throne
Not of this world
stand with Christ alone
Not of this world
be not of this world
until the trumpet is blown

YOUR WILL

Back and forth
Round and round
We give our best
Yet still we drown
When will we learn
there's a better way
When will we turn
Our pride away

Every will
can be right in our own mind
But is the will
Solid or just blind
Lord, if you will
Help me to find
The truth I seek
And help me see

Your will is bigger than ours
Help us see past our desires
Oh Lord,
how can we be
more like you
Your will of higher powers
Conquers all as it devours
Our sin
And sets us free
To be with you

Your will is bigger than ours
Your will of higher powers

Your will is bigger than ours
Help us see past our desires
Oh Lord,
how can we be
more like you
Your will of higher powers
Conquers all as it devours
Our sin
And sets us free
To be with you

Let your will be free
And flow though me

ANGEL VS DEMON

*Brother how could you fall
'Brother why did you stay
:How could you want it any other way

* You saw Him speak
and things come to exist
What's so enticing
you could not resist

* I saw Him aspire
And want the same for me
I admire His desire
To be more than created to be

: You force my hand against you
Your choice to take arms and fight
Prepare for war, I'm coming for you
You'll kneel and confess I'm right

: You're gonna be
** Cast out/locked in
: You're gonna be
** Locked out/has been
:Can't you see
No chance, we will win
Our eternity
Let it all begin
And we shall see

Brother look at this beauty
How can you turn it away
Brother you fail your duty
What about Judgment Day
You'll see who's victorious
Wish there could be another way

Brother, do you regret
The decision you made
Brother, I see
You're still afraid
You lost your chance
You can no longer trade

You see my army
You don't stand a chance
You see my army
And we'll take our stance
I see your army
Time to advance

Attaaaack...

You're gonna be
Washed out/done in
You're gonna be
Wiped out/has been
Can't you see
No chance, we will win
This eternity
Here we meet again
And we shall see

DOVE TO THE DEVIL

As 24/7 time flies by
what a difference a day can make
A flip of the coin and don't know why
Is it really all for goodness sake

One day can be a blessing
the next can be a curse
You can wonder
why you're stressing
then realize
it could be much worse

From Dove to the Devil
Oh how life can change
From Dove to the Devil
Life can rearrange
From the Dove to the Devil

Years ago a man came in
What a difference He would make
Said He could be forgiver of sin
and all would be for Heaven's sake

A day with John for Baptizing
then the desert to traverse
The Dove came down
with a voice of blessing
Then out to be tempted
by the Devil He must verse

From Dove to the Devil
Oh how life can change
From Dove to the Devil
Life can rearrange
From the Dove to the Devil

The Devil's a liar
And your soul he wants to take
Everything is to destroy
nothing for goodness sake

As a sheep he comes so deceiving
his intentions only to coerce
He thought he was winning
Then the resurrection broke the curse

From Dove to the Devil
Funny how life can change
From Dove to the Devil
A moment to rearrange
When the Dove beats the Devil

WORTH THE CLIMB

The more we focus on the past and the pain it brought,
the further enslaved and in the web we're caught.
If tears were able to carry away the hurt inside,
I'd be invincible and could raise my head with pride.
I can't say I wish the pains were never there,
they've helped me grow, help me love, and help me care.
Some pains prove I'm humble and some prove I'm tough,
but some break me down and tell me I'm not enough.
The enemy comes and tries to give us a fight,
but God assures us that our future is bright.
Even though we know all we have is today to see,
today is no guarantee of what tomorrow will be.
Even if today is the worst it's ever been,
tomorrow will be a fresh start to begin again.
When the time comes that tomorrow does not,
today's problems will not matter and be forgot.
All we can do is accept that it is what it is,
and figure out the best way to keep life's fizz.
We may need to shake it up a little more than before,
the other option is turn out the light and close the door.
Our pain doesn't go away if we choose to take that path, it
only transfer to the one's left behind in the aftermath.
There is always hope but it may take some time to find,
thinking there's no hope will drive you out of your mind.
The lights will come on when you flip the right switch, you
just have to keep going to find which is which.
Everything is temporary, just give it some time,
the view is always better after the long uphill climb.

LET GO

It was supposed to be simple
but my lack of wisdom lead me down the wrong path
A dark and twisted road that seems will dead end in wrath
The battle for front and center rages on driving me insane
It used to be just my mind
but now it's my heart with the agonizing pain
Either at anytime feels like one could bust
I know my life would be better if I could just

Let go
Of the struggle
Deep within me
Cuz it haunts me
Wanna let go
But I hold on

And it kills me
It's not easy
Letting go of all the pain deep inside me
When it grips me
When it harms me
Looking to the day I can be set free
The Misery
That's drowning me

Tired of how the pain
Keeps going on and on and on
Seems to have a mind all its own
Scary when left all alone
It's so controlling
And it's growing

I can't take it anymore
like waves crashing to the shore
Eroding away each drop of the sea
Take it all away before it all kills me

Let go
Let it all go
Why hold on
And go on
Holding on
Let it go
Let it all go

My child it's not for you to carry such pain
For what purpose did I become the lamb that was slain
Was it not so you could be forgiven
Repent, learn your lesson, and go on livin
Your pain will one day
make sense so let Me be in control
I know at times it won't make sense
but let me save your soul
You'll get to rule with me and listen to the Angels sing
But if you focus on your sorrows
only more suffering it will bring
The things you know now are only a temporary stay
Focus on me, I can make the pain go away

When you
Let go of the struggle
Deep within you
Cuz it harms you
You can let go
Why do you hold on
You know it kills you

So why go through
Holding on to all the pain deep inside you
It all harms you and it drains you
Why not open up your heart and just trust Me
Eternally
And be set free

No need for the pain
To keep going on and on and on
While having a mind all its own
Scary when left all alone
It's so controlling when it's growing
No need to take it anymore
like waves crashing to the shore
Eroding away each drop of the sea
Let it go and just trust in me

Let go
You can trust me
I'll forgive you
You're gonna have to
Put your trust in me
If you wanna be free

So let it go
You gotta let go
Let go all of all the sorrow
Deep inside you
So I can heal you
Of the struggle
Deep within you
Cuz it harms you
You can let go

You know it kills you
So why go through
Holding all the pain
That keep going on and on and on
While having a mind all its own
Scary when left all alone
It's so controlling
When it's growing
No need to take it anymore
like waves crashing to the shore
Eroding away each drop of the sea
Let it go and just trust in me

DARKNESS

Darkness
leaves me
helpless

Trapped alone I cannot hide
Truth be known, Truth's denied
Face my own Demon inside
Mind is blown, selfish pride

One day I had it all
Today I dropped the ball
No way to end this fall
Dismay, my worthless crawl

Is there
anyway out of
this Darkness
that leaves me
helpless

Choices made, what's the cost
Perceptions swayed, reality lost
Feelings fade, worth is tossed
Left afraid, feeling crossed

Left in regret, what can I do
Wish to forget, without a clue
Dead set on being through
Cold mindset, I wish I knew

How to escape
this darkness
that leaves me
helpless

PLEDGE ALLEGIANCE

I PLEDGE ALLEGIANCE

TO THE GOD WHO

CREATED THE UNIVERSE

AND TO HIS SON WHO DIED FOR US

ONE SAVIOR INCORRUPTIBLE

WHO WILL BE THE JUDGE OF ALL

FROM THE INSIDE

The world can be a scary place
Hard to deal when come face to face
With the struggles from afar that we trap within
Not knowing where to go or where to begin
Burdens pile up and weigh us down
Shoulders are strong but about to drown

Stop holding on to stuff on the inside
Let it go
Let it out
Ok to scream and shout
Let it be
Let it fly
Don't be afraid to cry
But stop holding all the stuff on the inside

The world can be a lovely place
When we learn to heal and learn to replace
All the struggles with love
All the pains within
Not knowing where to go or where to begin
Keeping the head up and reversing the frown
Facing the walls so you can tear them down

When we stop
Holding all the stuff on the inside
Let it go
Let it out
Ok to scream and shout

Let it be
Let it fly
Don't be afraid to cry
But stop holding all the stuff on the inside

False Evidence Appearing Real
Trying to change How I Feel
Escaping the trap set for me
Looking above to set them free

From the inside

Letting go of the stuff on the inside
Freeing myself from the inside

By stop holding on to stuff on the inside
Let it go
Let it out

WHILE IT LASTS

Eyes sprung open
Bewildered and amazed
What happened
Confused and dazed

Just yesterday it seems
I had life under control
But time has flown
and it has taken its toll

The beauty I admired
The tastes I devoured
No longer a treat
but wilted and soured

Enjoy it before you destroy it
the future will soon be the past
enjoy it while it last

I know giving something
won't get anything back
But what I still have
I need to keep on track
Moving ahead
without looking back
Enjoying the light
before it goes black

The times I treasure
That brought me pleasure
Fading fast
Losing its measure

With what I have left
I'm going to
Enjoy it before I destroy it
the future will soon be my past
Gonna enjoy it while it last

Memories of old slowly fade away
But making new memories every single day
Even though no longer the same
I've learned my lessons
And endured my shame

I'll continue to
Enjoy it before I destroy it
the future will soon be my past
Gonna enjoy it while it last

WANT TO GO

Death forever Death for real
Death for everyone to feel

Gone forever Gone for good
What I'm taught and understood

Am I right, Am I wrong
I know it wont be long

Eternally I will be
Faded memory

I hear you say I could be saved
Groundwork has been paved

Should I trust what I can't see
Is it Real or Fantasy

Yes I know
It's all I know
I don't wanna go

This fear I hide
tears me up inside
I go everyday
Choking on my pride

But I'll not let it show
I don't want to go

Free forever Free for real
Freedom only when I kneel

Saved forever Saved for good
Will you join, I wish you would

Are you right
Are you wrong
Forever is so long

Eternally
Will you be
Hand in hand with me

There's a way
To be saved
Redemption
Has been paved

Put your trust
In He
Who died
On Calvary

Yes I know
Now I know
I will wanna go

This peace inside
No longer can I hide
I go everyday
Thanking He who died

I'm not afraid to show
I will want to go

SATAN VS JESUS

Up from a slumber
deep in the Abyss
Roaring like thunder
slivering hiss

So little time
So much to do
I'll waste no time
destroying you

Waited so long
this final hour
Spread my wings
Weak will cower

Bow down
Confess to me
I'm your ruler of eternity
Stand up
Follow me
Working wonders in iniquity

I first came to the garden
to deceive
Stole the land God gave
To your Adam and Eve

I offered it back
for just one thing
worship me
as your king

All you weak
mortal man
Who cannot see
the immortal plan

Bow down
Confess to me
I'm your ruler of eternity
Stand up
Follow me
Working wonders in iniquity

Not being in charge
really set me off
But being kicked out
Really pissed me off
Ruler of a planet
Really rips me off
Defiling His creation
Really gets me off

I hate
all you're about
Just wait
Don't you doubt
I'll break
My Legion out
Mistake
About to hear Him shout

(Cont...)

Bow down
Confess to Me
I'm the Lord of eternity
Stand up
Depart from Me
You're the father of iniquity

You had your chance
And I proved you wrong
The Lake of Fire
That's where you belong

Your feeble attempts
At defeating Me
Only served My Will
I'm sure you'll agree

You served your purpose
and I thank you for that
You tried your best
but you've fallen flat

You left Me no choice
Gotta do what I said I would do
Too bad so many followed
May they forever torment you

Bow down
Confess to Me
I'm the King of eternity
Stand up
Depart from Me
All you workers of iniquity

HOLDING ON

Giving up
sometimes seems
like it's the best way out for me
When the pains and fears
from all the years
are the only thing I see

So many times
I've failed myself
and all the ones I love
And I fail to see
what good can come
from all I've dreamed of

A soft sweet voice
from deep within
whispers when all my hope is gone
You will see
what it means
if you just keep holding on

And I keep holding on
holding on
finding faith to make me strong
And I keep holding on
holding on
I pray oh God
it won't be long
But even if it is
I'll keep holding on

What's it for
what's it mean
I question it all everyday
When will it end
when will it mend
There has to be a better way

Patients are hard
and the future is dull
when now is all I can see
Help me oh Lord
give me a hand
help me believe in me

And keep me holding on
holding on
give me strength, make me strong
So I can keep holding on
Holding on
No matter what it takes
or how long
I ask you please
Keep me holding on

Whatever it takes
Whatever you need
No matter the pain
no matter the speed
Keep me holding on

You have a plan
I'm eager to know
Help me back up
and help me to grow
Keep me holding on

Keep me holding on
holding on
give me strength, make me strong
So I can keep holding on
Holding on
No matter what it takes
or how long
I ask you please
Keep me holding on

TEMPORARY

Like the sword
with the sharp double edge
Memories of a pain
Can heal or drive a wedge
Healing if the pain
taught a lesson never to repeat
But staying in the pain
can lead to ultimate defeat

There's a Savior who will forgive us
and ensure the pain won't last
But there's a Devil who likes to sneak in
and keep reminding of the past
I can't forget because the pain doesn't just affect me
Constantly reminded of the hurt in the loved ones I see

The only comfort I can live with
Is knowing in the end
All the pain will mean nothing
and forever I'll ascend
All these pleasures and the torments
won't mean a thing
Regardless where we're headed
all these things we cannot bring

It's all temporary
every moment every pleasure
It will all be lost
everything that we treasure
But without it now
how could we live
What could we take
how could we give

The here and now is all we have
we shouldn't take anything for granted
Though stuff shouldn't possess us
and make us feel so enchanted
The feeling of not good enough
slowly takes its toll
wish I could let go
of things beyond my control

I ache when I'm reminded
of how things are supposed to be
Drowning myself with distraction
seems to be the only working key
It helps to think the end of days
could soon be here
Though what if they are wrong
it's something I do fear

My gut tells me to go on
things will get better one day
I hope it's one day soon
so all this crap can go away
Day by day I'll push along
trying to do what's right
Hoping my heart goes on strong
staying to the end of the fight

THE BIBLE IS A LIE

There are a few very important questions to ask when it comes to this statement.
1: What would it take for a Bible believer to believe the Bible is a lie?
If the answer to this question is nothing, absolutely nothing can be shown, given, proven or any such thing to believe the Bible is a lie can you see how foolish, how closed minded, how arrogantly stubborn, how far into denialism they would be?
The 2nd Question:
What would it take for a nonbeliever to believe that it's NOT a lie?
Can you see that if the same NOTHING answer is given, then same foolish, closed minded, arrogant stubbornness denialism applies?
Why are people soooo set in their ways that they simply refuse to believe anything other than what they currently believe?

Why do YOU think it's True or Lie?
Can you agree on how irresponsible it is to say the Bible is True or Lie based solely on someone else's opinion or teaching? If you've not read the Bible and done any History research or tried to apply its teaching, then you have no place to say it's not true. Same goes for those who haven't read it and say it is true...Though the most important question with this is...

Who does it matter to more if they are wrong?
The Bible believers if it's a lie
OR
Nonbelievers if it's true?
This is not about whether the Bible is complete or not, whether it's misunderstood or not, or whether it's applicable to today's society or not...what would it take for you as a person to let go of what you thought was true for so long and accept something else?
It will not matter for Bible believers. IF we are reincarnated as a lot of different religions believe, then we'll get to come back to try again. IF it's nothing after we die, then it doesn't matter. But it will matter for everyone if there is a Heaven and Hell!

MATTER OF PERSPECTIVE
In a Universe of opposing arguments someone has to be wrong...yes, it could be no one is right, but someone is absolutely wrong.
When our Self-Will is the driving force, it can seem as though everyone can be right.
When there is a Creator with a Devine-Will, then there will be people wrong as long as they go against it.
Though it's funny how people will complain about the Bible is written by man but will follow other books known for certain to be written by man.
IS THERE A GOD OR NOT....
AT HE IS T [HE IS AT the T (cross)

It would be understandable that people wouldn't want to believe the Bible if Jesus was teaching us to kill anyone that simply refused to accept His teaching or kill anyone who decides to no longer follow His teaching anymore.

How crazy it is that society does actually accept someone who is just like that, but yet curses someone who preaches love.

The Quran began some 500 years after the Bible ended and is pretty much just the opposite of it...yet this is how society treats them.

Fortunately, many Muslims and Atheists are leaving their faith for one that actually is of Love and becoming what the World sees as the greatest threat to the world.

If the Bible is a lie, how can someone sell their soul to the Devil/Satan and get Earthly riches on such a regular basis?

If reincarnation is real and Christians now are wrong, then we'll get to come back for another chance.

If Reincarnationist are wrong, they will not.

If it's nothing, then it matters to no one. If it's something, it matters to everyone wrong.

We are ALL only guaranteed now. This is what we see and this is what we can touch...we are all putting faith into what comes next.

For me it will take at least more evidence than I have now to outweigh my belief that the Bible is NOT a lie.

A Theist vs Atheist

The word atheist is just like an inverted Cross commonly associate with Satanism or any mockery of the Crucifixion of Jesus, as well as the LGBT's distortion of the Rainbow. The upside down cross or mocking of the Crucifixion still implies to the followers that there is a Right side up...a Savior. The number 6 identifies man and Self-Will and 7 represents Completion/Perfection and God's Will. The original Rainbow was given as a Covenant between God and the few people who listened to Him that the World would never be destroyed by flood again, which every culture has stories of a worldwide flood. Removing a color shows rebellion, Straightening the bow shows defiance Removing GOD, the only color of the visible 7 color spectrum that has GOD in it...INDIGO is

GOD IN I,

(only in some of the flags) shows self-righteousness. They are all admitting there is truth, but showing the rejection of it... People are not ignorant of the truth. but are in willful rebellion of it.

In the Garden of Eden, the Serpent used the same cunning skills that are still used to this day, and so many people still fall for it.

Christian...one who wants to be like Christ. What did Jesus do that has so many hating Him so much?

Didn't He preach to love your neighbors as yourself? To turn the other cheek if attacked? Isn't His message one of love? To give your coat if asked for a shirt?

To love your enemy and pray for those who persecute you?

Jesus is the most powerful name in the Universe So again, why do people hate him so much?

It seems like when anti-Christian people speak and throw Bible verses out, it's about Old Testament scripture. As far as what we have about Jesus, what did He have to do with the stories in the Old Testament?

It's one thing to want to believe He's just a profit or did not exist. but it's another thing to come out and hate, attack, and mock Him... Why is that? Why do YOU hate Jesus? Forget about the Christians who are sinful people needing a redeemer and things that they've done to give Christianity a bad name, but why do YOU hate Jesus?

LET'EM RIDE

Let'em ride
Let'em riide
Let'em riiide

Oh, Let'em ride
Let'em riide
Let'em riiide

Let the horsemen ride

The stables must be ready
and the riders mounted in
Gallup riding steady
Riding in the wind

It's been a long time we've been waiting
And still wait patiently await
No more point and blaming
Open up the gate

It seems were long overdue
But it's up to you
When you let'em ride
But when you are through
We will know it was you
When you let'em ride

Let'em ride-Let'em ride-Let'em riiide
Oh, Let'em ride-Let'em ride-Let'em riiide
Let the horsemen ride

The first horse comes to conquer
And the second bringing war
The third comes with famine
And the last brings hell to the door

One at a time the world will see
Why this all must be done
They'll say to themselves, how can this be
We rejected the chosen one

We're so long overdue
But it's up to you
When you let'em ride
But when you are through
We will know it was you
When you let'em ride

Let'em ride
Let'em riide
Let'em riiide

Oh, Let'em ride
Let'em riide
Let'em riiide

Let the horsemen ride

Give us strength
until we get to the other side
Let'em come just as they are
But let the horsemen ride

LET IT BE YOURS

Some days are good
Some days are bad
A genie in a bottle I wish I had
So many lessons to learn
Too many mistakes to be made
The fight's been strong
but I'm starting to fade

I've been
Leaning on my own understanding
Turning away the hand you keep handing
Stuck in a quest I've been searching for

Struggling through life all so demanding
In a search that seems is never ending
The more I get, I'm only wanting more

God, I know my yesterday's gone
And I stand here today, all alone
Asking you Lord
Save me from my tomorrow
Please save me from my tomorrow
And let it be yours

Do I continue the path
I've been headed down
Or give it all up
And just turn around
What am I doing right
What changes should I make
Give me a sign
There's so much at stake

I know I've been
Leaning on my own understanding
Turning away the hand you keep handing
Stuck in a quest I've been searching for

Struggling through life all so demanding
In a search that seems is never ending
The more I get, I'm only wanting more

God, I know my yesterday's gone
And I stand here today, all alone
Asking you Lord
Save me from my tomorrow
Please save me from my tomorrow
And let it be yours
Let it be yours
Oh, let it be yours

WHAT'S WRONG

When you find yourself asking
what's wrong with the world
how can it be so bad
What's up with all the hatred
why in the world
does it have to be so sad

Know there's a plan that's been laid out
Through the centuries has been Played out
Not one thing left undone
So many people have sold out
So many more wanting to hold out
The end told before it began

We've read the book
We know it ends
Take a good look
Tell all your friends
The end is among us
but be not afraid
A judgment awaits us
Though the debt has been paid
For those who believe
the path has been paved
for those who believe

The Word has been around
since the Creation of time
It spells it all out
all of history
A redeemer being punished
without a crime
and a deceiver on the lose
with a cunning conspiracy

Go read the book
and tell all your friends
Take a good look
to see how it ends
The end is among us
but be not afraid
A judgment awaits us
Though the debt has been paid
For those who believe
the path has been paved
for those who believe

Every thought, every deed
Every gift, every greed
A coming judgement awaits

Every word, every prayer
Every curse, every swear
Then off through the gates

Heaven or hell
no in between
It's all loving and fair
even if you think it's mean
Most won't agree and will think it's unjust
but the creator makes the rules
and to be fair He must
Lay it all out and let you choose
It's your soul to gain
it's your soul to lose
Accept or reject it
the debt has still been paid
will you be forever happy
with the choice you made

It's all been paid
for those who believe
it's up to you
you can receive
Give it a chance
set yourself free
Doesn't take much
you can be
With those who believe
debt has been paid
for those who believe

WAR

Tempers rising all across the land
The World dividing seems to be the plan
Why in the world are we so ungrateful
We can be better than this
Why in the World do we have to be so hateful
Are we all being betrayed with a kiss

Temperature rising all across the land
Climate changing is that part of the plan
Something is coming
Something we can't dismiss
Disaster is coming
But the world is lost in a bliss

There's gonna be war
War, war after rumor of war
Worldwide war
Every shore
Are you ready for this war

I say, Let it rain, Let it pour
Bring on your final war
Because this war
This war
Will be the turning war
To bring Christ's reign
and His reign
is what I'm waiting for

It's not bad news
It's not sad news
But it goes against the world views

The ones with issues
are those who refuse
The Word of God and His good news

What's with the ego
It's your choice to choose
War is coming
What's with the ego
What do you have to lose
War is coming
Let the ego take a little bruise
Because war is coming

When ya gonna see the reality
The Bible is the blueprint, it is the key
Everything is going just like it said
and your creator awaits you after you're dead.

There's gonna be war
War, war after rumor of war
Worldwide war
Every shore
Are you ready for this war

And I say, Let it rain, Let it pour
Bring on your final war
Because this war
This war
Will be the turning war
To bring Christ's reign
and His reign
is what I'm waiting for

MAN ON A MISSION

A Man on a mission
a God with a vision
Good and evil head on collision
Tree of knowledge, good, and evil
Stay away or unleash upheaval
The crushing of your head
will bring bruising of His heel
you'll think you'll won
when you take Him to the hill

Break out the hammer
Bring out the nails
Break out the hammer
This man condemned himself
Bring out the hammer
Break out some nails
Bring out the hammer
The justice weighted scales

The disciples knew the truth
but did not comprehend
Pharisees despised the truth
And wanted it to end
The cross was not a curse
or meant for punishment
It was the Will if God
soon to finish the reason He was sent

Now that I know
Now I understand
You're not just a god
nor just a man

Give me the hammer
hand me some nails
Hand me the hammer
I'll nail you up myself
Hand me the hammer
Give me some nails
Give me the hammer
To watch the serpent shed his scales

Break out the hammer
bring out the nails
Give me the hammer

Bring out the hammer
Break out the nails
Hand me the hammer

Give me the hammer
and hand me the nails
Let me do the Will of God
and deny my own self
Hand me the hammer
Give me some nails
So You can bring Your hammer
To bring justice weighted scales

WAITING

So many centuries
have come and gone
So many believers
still going on
We've been told to wait
but how much longer
Evil surrounds us
and is growing stronger

Lord, we're waiting
We're praying
Anticipating
For your return
or you call us home
Either way beck to your throne
Until then
give us strength to
keep waiting
keep praying
Anticipating

Quickly I come
we seem to disagree
Generations have vanished
but now so many signs to see
Dates have been set
setters have been mocked
Though I know one day
the world will be shocked

Your will

We're waiting
We're praying
Anticipating
For your return
or you call us home
Either way beck to your throne
Until then
give us strength to
keep waiting
keep praying
Anticipating

Give us strength
and understanding
Let us hear
what you're commanding
Keep us safe
keep us yearning
May we live
For your returning

As we keep waiting
and praying
Anticipating

EMBRACING GOD'S ALMIGHTY LOVE EVERYDAY

CAN'T HELP BUT WONDER

Everything's great
Everything's fine
I've got all I need
Everything's in line
I've got sports on the tv
Cool beats in my ears
I have food on the table
and good friends for cheers

Though there's something missing
Something's just not right
I have all I've wanted
Yet something keeps me up at night

I can't help but
wonder wonder wonder
What could it be
It keeps pulling me
Under under under
The pressure drowning me

It's sounds like
Thunder thunder thunder
On some killing spree
It's tearing at me
Sunder sunder sunder
Feels like it's crushing me

Everything now
is falling apart
All the stuff is gone
and a broken heart
Where did I go wrong
what did I do
What did I do wrong
I haven't a clue

I find my mind
fills more and more
With pleasures and fear
like never before
The ups and downs
getting further apart
The downs drag on
Is it time to depart

I keep falling falling falling
Crying God will you please
Keep me from
Falling falling falling
God do you hear my pleas

I'm now
calling calling calling
Down on my knees
Here I am
Crawling crawling crawling
God will you help me please

Sorry I left you
out of my life
I know that I need you
Whether tranquil or strife
All the stuff means nothing
I can't bring it along
Forgive me my trespass
and help me stand up strong

Keep me now
praising praising praising
Your glorious name
I'll keep on
Praising praising praising
Until you call my name

It was you
calling calling calling
Calling out for me
I can't help but
Bawling bawling bawling
Now that you've rescued me

BRING IT ALL DOWN

Empires rise and empires fall
History repeats and affects us all
Statues erect of the very elect
Hidden agenda hard to detect
A kingdom awaits we've yet to see
Echoed through out all eternity

It wasn't meant to last
only meant to serve
A kingdom of grace
we don't deserve
Ruled by the One who wears the crown
The world awaits until you bring the kingdom down

Bring it all down
Until your feet hit the ground
Bring it all down

With every blow of the hammer
Slamming on the nail
You knew they knew not
Yet would forgive them and defeat hell
With the piercing of the thorns
deep into your head
You knew it was only your body that would soon be dead
Then it was finished with the piercing of the spear
Then came the flood of both blood and tear

Bring it all down
Until every drop hits the ground
Bring it all down

Now ere are here, the statue is complete
Waiting for the stone to come crash at the feet
You said when you were here not one stone would be left on another
We're waiting for you since salvation is found in no other
Much blood has been shed and tears overflow
Your Kingdom comes when only you know

Bring it all down
Until everything has hit the ground
Bring it all down

SWEET LOVE

My heart had been troubled
With everything going on
My mind keeps racing
Wondering if it's too far gone

Wish my prayers helped me through the day
A little more than they do
The pain seems like it's here to stay
But then I get to come home to you

You are my sweet love-my saving grace
So thankful you're always here with me
You warm my soul when I see your face
And I know that without you I rather not be

We've been through some ups,
been through some downs
Found grace from our Lord up in the sky
But sometimes you need a touch
through tears and frowns
And I'll treasure your touch til the day I die

You are my sweet love-my saving grace
So thankful you're always here with me
You warm my soul when I see your face
And I know that without you I rather not be

You are my sweet love-my saving grace
So thankful you're always here with me
You warm my soul when I see your face
And I know that without you I rather not be

My sweet love, my saving grace
Oh yes you are my sweet love
My saving grace
Such a sweet touch
When I see your face
Thank you for your sweet touch
My saving grace

FRACTIONED TIME

A fraction in time
is all it takes
To feel the reward
or make our mistakes
Each moment we have
is not like the last
With each beat of the heart
they're a thing of the past
So why do we take
moments for granted
Why so many times
we wish were recanted

Please can I take back
the words I didn't mean them
Feeling attacked
and lost in the moment

Please can we go back
To before I expressed them
To have it all back
If just for a moment
I was lost in the moment

The hands of time
will pass like the wind
Vanishing reality
but will the time mend
The damages done
to the heart and the soul
And give healing to
all that pain stole
The power of the tongue
can speak life or death
Some words are regretted
with every last breath

Treasure each moment
You don't know
when it will be your last

Please can I take back
the words I didn't mean them
Feeling attacked
and lost in the moment

Please can we go back
To before I expressed them
To have it all back
If just for a moment
I was lost in the moment

PERCEPTION

Circumstances have a way of dictating how we feel
And evidence surrounding says it must be real
But our eyes can be tricked, and our hearts deceived
While perception and fear make a mess
in the web we've weaved
Perception is reality only to the eyes of the beholder
And facts of the matter can be lost in a blunder

It's hard to keep your head up
When so many things are pulling you down
It's easy just to give up
Feeling alone with no one around
That's the time you need to look up
And pray God's love and be found
And feel a little cheer up
Knowing God's love is always abound

Looking back on something allows us the 20/20 know
And gives clarity while making room for us to grow
Nothing can be built without dedication and action
Though more may be needed when there's a painful distraction
Some projects may be slower than we think they should be
But everything always works out for the good, just wait and see

It's hard to keep your head up
When so many things are pulling you down
It's easy just to give up
Feeling alone with no one around
That's the time you need to look up
And pray God's love and be found
And feel a little cheer up
Knowing God's love is always abound

LAY IT ALL OUT

Someday
this all will end
And everything we ever were
will just be dust in the wind

That day
Will be shared by all
So what can we do now
before God makes that call

We only have one life to live
So much to do only so much to give

While we are here
While we're alive
While we're all breathing and we're able
lay it all out on the table
You're gonna mistakes
and that's ok
With enough time
they'll all be washed away
So lay it all out

Keep in mind
Others around you
Everyone's journey a different story
Meshing together like drops in a sea
Only make promises you can keep
Remember harsh words really cut deep

While we are here
While we're alive
While we're all breathing and we're able
lay it all out on the table
You're gonna mistakes
and that's ok
With enough time
they'll all be washed away

So lay it all out
Lay it all out
Lay it all out

Don't let it be good or bad
Just an experience that you had
Learn from the lesson and carry on
One day soon it'll all be gone

While we are here
While we're alive
While we're all breathing and we're able
lay it all out on the table
You're gonna mistakes
and that's ok
With enough time
they'll all be washed away

So lay it all out
Lay it all out
Lay it all out
Everything you've got
Lay it all out

THE VILOLATED

If you ask me how I feel
I'll say I'm doing fine
But if I have to be for real
Just gonna keep those feelings mine
There are a few that help me keep my sanity in tact
But for the masses around
so sick of how they act

I'll help and I'll give because
that's just who I am
But more and more these days
I just don't give a damn
The gallows should be reopened
and they should all be full
One last door and a fatal lever
I would gladly volunteer to pull

The agenda of mental madness
pushed on us at every turn
There needs to be a cleansing
we need to see some evil burn
But who would it be, I hate to admit
the list is pretty long
If you have to coerce, deceive, or hide your intent,
it's you who belong

But it's not my fight and it's not a war
that I'm big enough to wage
Holding on to the hope
the Savior will soon take the stage

I CANT

I can't think about the things I wish I had
I can't focus on the things I wish I would've done better
It's too hard
I can't reflect back on the mistakes I've made
I can't reminisce of the good things I used to have
It's too sad

I can't continue to beat myself up for the times I feel I failed
I can't persevere if I keep falling into the same pitfalls
It's too depressing
I can't maintain sanity trying to control the things that can't be controlled
I can't go forward caring all the burdens
I let myself get trapped under
It's too oppressing

I can't ignore the purpose it seems God chose for me
I can't fathom the complexity that goes
into making the improbable possible
There's more than a mystery

I can't how many things I missed before having eyes to see
I can't dismiss the patterns that repeat in headlines and events
There's proof all throughout history

I can't fail to realize that never falling is what makes one a failure
I can't give up when something doesn't go as planned
There's too much at stake
I can't turn my back on those who have been there for me
I can't abandon the handful of people I love more than myself
There's more memories to make

ROLLERCOASTER

Life can be a crazy rollercoaster
and people all around can make it harder
I wish the world was a little bit safer
and pain in my heart a little bit softer

What can I do
What should I do

Cuz
I get little scared
and I feel hollow
And sometimes the truth
Is hard to swallow~
It's hard when it's only me
Lord
They say You're greater than
all my sorrow
Please will You save me
from my tomorrow
Please Lord deliver me

Thank you Lord
I'm feeling much better
Can't believe
I didn't do this sooner
I can forgive myself
and feel much freer
Since you forgiven me
Became my redeemer

Now
No need to fear
or feeling hollow
Deliver the truth
Easy to swallow~
It's hard when it's only me
Lord
You are greater than
all my sorrow
You've taken care of
My tomorrow~
Lord you delivered me

Now even when I'm feeling down
I still know you're around
I don't have to look very far
Call your name and there you are

It's not easy letting go
But one thing I've come to know
Your Word is forever true
and we're nothing without you

LET ME OUT

Brick by brick
Layer by layer
Walls are built
To let nothing in

A sealant is set
Holes are filled
Then all reinforced
Ensure nothing comes in

Time passes by
Reasons for walls
Pass away too
Still nothing comes in

Wanting to come out
The walls are too thick
What can you do
To let something in

Tearing them down
Takes twice as long
Will it be possible
To let someone in

It seems as though
Once they are built
There's no way out
Forever stuck within

MY TIME

Each day I live I have a choice
each day alive I have a voice
I can live in clattered noise
or give praise and rejoice

Each day I give a part of me
each day I choose who I will be
I can live in misery
or take control and be free

I have but one life to live
only have one heart to give
What is good is relative
do we hold a grudge or forgive

I don't know when I'm gonna die
could be any moment that passes by
I can accept God's grace or deny
bow my head in shame or lift it to the sky

I can't be the only one who thinks time is special
I can't be the only one who thinks time is crucial
Cherish your time and make it useful
Every moment counts
don't make them wasteful

It's time I take time by the hand
This time I want to understand
Time disappears with each drop of sand
I'm the only one who can take command
Of my time

LET ME SLEEP

Deep in the REM I spread my wings and fly
Deep in the REM neither live nor die
Paranoia euphoria wrapped into one
Consistence nonexistence, let's have some fun

They look at us like we're so better off
Little do they know we gotta turn and cough
Build it big, build it high no matter the cost
Point and blame, all the same, none is lost

It feels so real
all so real
it must be true
Though a strange request
I must ask of you

Don't pinch me
Don't wake me up
Don't pinch me
let me sleep
Don't pinch me
Do not disturb
Don't pinch me
Just let me be

Happy in my world I created just for me
Boogie-men don't exist in my reality
Don't pinch me
Just let me be

No need to know
what's going on
I'm good to go 'til the end of dawn
Let me be

One day,
one life,
one eternity
Doesn't really matter;
all the same to me

I don't even care what you have to say
I'm gonna think what I want to anyway
So take my advice and listen to me
Just leave me alone and let me be

Let me sleep

Don't pinch me
Don't wake me up
Don't pinch me
let me sleep
Don't pinch me
Don't disturb me
Don't pinch me
Just let me be

NOTHING

I'm sorry that who I am
isn't who you want me to be

I'm sorry that who you are
isn't who I want you to be

We share the same blood and same name
and for that I'm sorry

I am a person that can see
Nothing good ever will bless me
I am the person I need to be
Nothing weak will ever break me
I am my own worst enemy
Nothing but hate consumes me
I am the person you made me

I'm sorry you'll never get the chance to make it up to me
I'm sorry I wasn't good enough
for you to be proud of me

We share the same ground but you're on the other side
and for that I'm sorry

You are the person
who always gave me
Nothing
not even love to me
You are a person
now dead to me
Nothing you can do to help me
You are the person
who taught me
Nothing
Nothing good from you lives in me
You are the person who made me

I'm sorry you can't see
me be more of a man
than you could ever be
I'm sorry I have to go on hating and running to stay free
We share a common enemy that I'm prepared to fight
and for that
I'm sorry

WHEN THE RAIN COMES

There's a storm cloud in the distance
and it looks like it's going to rain
We probably should go inside
before it's too late and avoid its pain.

It might not come this way
but we've been caught before
What can we better do to avoid
the tremendous down pour?

Unfortunately, we have been caught
unexpected and felt the wrath
Though eventually we'll learn
all the signs to stay on the right path.

If the rain didn't sting so much
we could stay out and play
But sometimes it's a little too much
and we just need to get away.

Thank God most days
are sunny with no rain in sight
How awesome it is to sit under the stars
and watch the twinkling light.

Though when the rain comes
I know it won't last very long
And the returning light will expose
anything that may be wrong.

If we're lucky we'll get
to see the rainbow in the sky
And we'll get to hold each other
tight while all nice and dry.

I don't look forward to the rain
but I know it may be needed
I know the harvest will flourish
with all that we've seeded.

I look forward to the harvest
when we get to reap what we sow
And no matter the weather that comes
just know I love you so.

THINGS IN LIFE

There are things in life
we wish we could undo
Bad things in life
if only we knew
Going back to correct a wrong
to maybe help life along

Harsh words or things handled bad
misunderstanding and feeling sad
How would it be if we knew it all before
would we want the same or want even more

Then there are things in life
we wish we could redo
Great things in life
again, would like to go through
Going back to relive something great
with more rocks in the bowl to accumulate

Fun times and precious moments shared
the world could be ending and neither cared
How would it be if we never met
would it be a life we would always regret

Wondering how it would've been
if given a chance to do it all again
One thing I know as I think it through
if I could do it again, I'd do all again with you

OLD AND GREY

When the time has come and we're old and grey
and we sit upon our swing
With our birds and dogs running around
not worried about a thing

We'll have lived a life as it was meant to live
Forever you and I
Knowing there was nothing else more we could give
Forever you and I

The sands in the glass fall as the should
every grain destined for an appointed time
Some fall fast some fall slow
some will clash but most whistle & chime

Whatever the cause
regardless the reason
We'll make through
anytime of season

Until that day, we get to laugh and play
Forever you and I
Getting to live and learn every day
Forever you and I

With love for each other we can move forward and shine
happily knowing I am yours and you are mine
Forever you and I

NOT MY INTENTION

What's the point what's it for
why do we even bother
Imperfections abound
and plague one another
There is a purpose we have
to each is own
Still praying the whys
are one day known
I have my flaws
but yet I try
It's still not right
and I don't know why

It was
Never my intentions
to bring you pain
All I ever wanted
was you to be proud of me
Some choices I've made
I know have left a stain
It kills me to see you hurt
I pray one day you see
-It was never my intension

It's not fair to you
when I don't know what you mean
The consequences now
I wish I could've seen
Back before all the things
went so wrong
The hell going through
Seems to be so long

I wish you could forgive me
Hope to prove I'm sorry

I never ever wanted
to bring us harm
We know some strains
Just a false alarm
What if we could stop
the emotional ride
Be understanding
and swallow some pride

It was
Never my intentions
to bring you pain
All I ever wanted
was you to be proud of me
Some choices I've made
I know have left a stain
It kills me to see you hurt
I pray one day you see
-It was never my intension

Wanting the best for you
my intention
Being there for you
my intention
Always loving you
my intention
But bring harm to you
was never my intention

MILESTONES

Milestones are markers, not of destination but
In progression or accomplishments in
Life. Unfortunately time does not reflect or
Encourage milestones as we age. How old
Someone is does not guarantee progression. It
Takes hard lessons sometimes while other times
Only wisdom or guidance from someone else
Not close to the situation to turn on the lights or
Encourage a different way of thinking when
Sadness, failure, or other such negative emotions
Take our joy away. We have been through
Our fair share of milestones in life before
Getting together as well as with each other.
Each milestone is set for different people
To reach at different times and in different ways.
Having the patience for our own milestones can be
Extremely difficult and waiting for others to
Reach certain expected milestones can
Feel discouraging and overwhelming. It's
Our job to help when we can but also the
Responsibility of each person to look within
Every aspect of their life and want to be better.
Very few people seem to want this but with
Each other, we are learning well how to
Resolve the issues that have been holding us back.
We have come a long way but our journey
Is nowhere close to being over. I look forward
To our future together regardless of
How many people don't want to share it.
You are my love and I am grateful for each
Of the milestones we've reached together even
Under some very hard circumstances.

Other books by:

Michael Massanelli

Hear My Songs of Praise
My Shattered Rose Colored Glasses
Just Remember...Jesus Love You

Coded Critters Activity Book 1-4
Coded Critters Coloring Book
Coded Critters Full Color Book

Stretching Revolution

(Available at Amazon)
or
www.MichaelMassanelli.com

MASSANELLI 4X4

Made in the USA
Monee, IL
26 April 2023